Published by Truth Publications, LLC
www.truth-brand.com
Illustrated by Tullip Studio

My Mimi is the Mayor
ISBN: 978-1-7366112-6-5
Copyright ©2022 by Veronica Smith-Creer
www.mayor-sunshine.com
All Rights Reserved

*To my daughter, VaShaylia Brianne Creer,
the first little girl to ever steal my heart.*

My name is Skylar,
and I am four.
Come see what my Mimi
and I have in store.

My Mimi stays busy, but that is okay!
She always makes time to laugh and play!

Her office is big with a spinning chair!
I have so much fun when I visit her there!

My Mimi takes me to lots of places!
I love to see all the smiling faces!

Sometimes to meetings. Those are fun, too!
I like being introduced to everyone new!

**Her outfits are colorful and pretty!
She stands out from the rest!**

Especially when I am with her. Those times are the best!

My Mimi is the Mayor.
The first to be a lady!
She told me she made
HERStory,
but it has been
that way since
I was a baby.

MAYOR

Interview with *Michelle Obama*

My Mimi said **HERStory** is showing what women can do.

She said, "You can be great and still be naturally you."

My Mimi told me that I would see more.
Then, the Vice President of the United States
and a Supreme Court Justice did it
before I turned four.

Yes, she is the Mayor, but she is my Mimi too!

Here are some of the fun things we get to do!

**We read books out loud
and play lots of games!**

We watch TV and sing songs!
No day is the same!

We laugh!
We act silly!
The fun
doesn't stop!

We go to parks, restaurants,
and shop around the square.

But my all-time favorite is combing her hair!

She said
I could be
whatever
I want.

Reader's Reflection

Who were the main characters?

What are some of the activities that Skylar does with her Mimi?

Of all the activities Skylar does with her Mimi, which is Skylar's favorite?

What do you think Mimi meant when she told Skylar that she would see more of HER story being made?

Did Skylar see more of HER story being made? How?

Skylar said her Mimi stands out from the rest. What other pages had characters that stood out (or did not look the same as those around them)?

I would like to dedicate this book to the first little girl to ever steal my heart, my daughter, VaShaylia Brianne Creer. You taught me more than you will ever know by being my greatest gift and my prayers personified! Being a mother has been one of the most fulfilling jobs I have ever possessed!

Throughout your childhood you had to attend a lot of meetings and several events because I wanted you to see what your Mommy was doing. I hoped that it would have an impact on your life. I think it did! I will never forget your sincere objection to me running for mayor. You did not want me to be criticized or demeaned. I am still in awe of you wanting to protect me. As we reach the end of this term, I know we both have matured and developed more patience.

This book is reminiscent of the promise I made to you over four years ago. The Movement was about not only you and the other young ladies coming behind me, but it was also for the babies yet to be born and ladies my age. Thank you for believing in your Mommy even when it looked like the odds were against me! Your faith in God is beautiful!

Your mother has served a lot of roles, but I am proudest for being just that, your mother!

About the Author:

Veronica Smith-Creer is an African American woman and has been married to Bobby D. Creer since April 20, 1996. Together they have three children; Bobby Jr., Jeremy Ryan, and VaShaylia Brianne, as well as two grandchildren; Jhavon Isiah and Skylar Brielle. Veronica has enjoyed life in El Dorado almost her entire life. Community service and volunteering have been at the forefront of her personal life for many years along with a love for public speaking and writing.

Mrs. Smith-Creer is currently serving in the position of Mayor in El Dorado, AR. Elected in November 2018, she became the first woman and first person of color to ever be elected as mayor in her hometown! It was the beginning of HERStory and the continuation of the Movement! Not only was the election monumental for her, but it also produced a platform that had never existed in her city before. She was the example of being the first for many!

A Message from the Author:

It is my desire that this book will serve as a reminder that the life you lead now will be the path the next generation will follow. Take the time to ensure you are preparing them for success by simply embracing the fact that there are options to who and what they can be! "My Mimi is the Mayor" is inspired by the relationship Skylar and I have created. At only four years old, I have been the mayor her entire life! The truth is, that title is not nearly as important to her as the title of being her Mimi!

Made in the USA
Las Vegas, NV
10 November 2023

80490576R00019